ACKNOWLEDGEMENT OF THE LAND AND FAITH OF ABORIGINAL CUSTODIANS AFTER FOLLOWING THE ABRAHAM TRAIL

NORMAN HABEL

a. Acorn Press

Published by Acorn Press
An imprint of Bible Society Australia
ACN 148 058 306 | Charity licence 19 000 528
GPO Box 4161
Sydney NSW 2001
Australia
www.acornpress.net.au | www.biblesociety.org.au

ISBN 978-0-647-53338-3

First published by Morning Star Publishing in 2018,
ISBN 978-0-648-23239-1

NATIONAL LIBRARY OF AUSTRALIA

A catalogue record for this work is available from the National Library of Australia

Cover and text design and layout by John Healy

Contents

Invitation

Your Church, Organisation or Community

is invited to follow

THE ABRAHAM TRAIL

outlined in this volume

and make an

Acknowledgement

— of —

THE LAND AND FAITH OF
THE ABORIGINAL CUSTODIANS

in your Country

Preface

The Abraham Trail

I have followed the Abraham trail many times during my life, perusing the original Hebrew language, the ancient Abraham legend and the rich Canaanite culture.

I have followed the trail with students, sceptics and biblical scholars. I have also followed the trail closely with my Aboriginal mentor and elder, George Rosendale, and with other Australian Aborigines such as Ivan Copley.

In recent years, as I followed the trail of my great grandfather who came to Australia as a refugee in the 1850s, I listened afresh to the story of how my Aboriginal brothers and sisters were treated when Europeans migrants and missionaries first entered this land of promise. Finally, I sought to read the text of the Abraham trail with new eyes—the eyes of the Aboriginal Peoples in Canaan.

What I discovered was rather frightening, but significant in the contemporary context of acknowledging the land by establishing a treaty relationship with the Aboriginal custodians of the land.

I am a descendant of a Prussian migrant who can be compared to Abraham who moved from his homeland, Ur of the Chaldees, to the host country of Canaan. And the Aboriginal peoples of Canaan can be compared to the Aboriginal Peoples in the land of Australia and other countries.

If I now follow the Abraham trail with my great grandfather and meet with the Canaanites who welcomed Abraham into their land, what might I discover along the Abraham trail? And if my Aboriginal mentors walk the trail with me, what are the events on the trail that might be relevant for life with Aboriginal Peoples today?

The text embracing the Abraham legend has been read, over the centuries, by a wide range of interpreters each from his/her own perspective. The first of these were the Israelite narrators of Genesis who lived several hundred years after the days of Abraham—narrators who read from an Israelite-Promised-Land perspective.

Writers like St Paul saw the promises addressed to Abraham fulfilled in a radically different way—a spiritual way. For St Paul, Abraham's acceptance of God's promises made Abraham a gentile 'man of faith' like those who believed in the promises of the Christian Gospel.

Recent generations of colonial readers have viewed the promised land tradition of the narrator of the Abraham trail as divine justification for entry into so-called uncivilised lands of the New World: lands like Australia, America and South Africa.

My goal is to travel back to the original Abraham trail to uncover—as far as possible—the primal faith, experience of land and vision of Abraham as the forefather of our Western tradition, the vision of a genuine land, faith and treaty relationship with the custodians of Canaan.

That a Canaanite interpretation of the original promise of land given to Abraham is relevant and painful for me today is evident from a memorial to the families—including my relatives—who settled in the Barossa Valley in South Australia. The biblical text quoted on the memorial is,

THE LORD HAS GIVEN US THIS LAND.

THE LORD HAS GIVEN US THIS LAND. Joshua 2.9.

BAROSSA PIONEER MEMORIAL

1842 — 1992

These words, believed to have been spoken by Joshua, are appropriated as being fulfilled a second time when the Germans settled the Barossa Valley. If the land of South Australia is equivalent to Canaan, then the Aboriginal inhabitants of the Barossa are apparently equivalent to the Canaanites who could be dispossessed by the invading German settlers.

Ironically, the craftsmen who prepared this memorial gave the wrong reference (Jos. 2.10) for the text cited. The person speaking the words cited was none other than Rahab the harlot, the Canaanite who welcomed the Israelite spies.

In spite of memorials such as the above and the frequent treatment of the Aboriginal Peoples as the 'Canaanites' in the land, I hope that by retracing the early steps of Abraham along the Abraham trail I may unearth an alternative tradition that will provide a basis for positive relationships between the settlers and the custodians of this land—a basis grounded in the spiritual world of the Aboriginal peoples of Canaan and those of the land down under.

I am well aware that over the years scholars have identified several narrators, often called redactors, who have edited stories from the Abraham legend from various perspectives and that the final edition of the Abraham narrative may have been as late as the exile (Habel, 1971).

I believe, however, that by exploring the early Abraham traditions preserved and reformulated by these narrators, it is possible to retrieve the primal faith and experience of Abraham that can provide us with a precedent and motivation

. for relating positively to the Aboriginal Peoples as the traditional custodians of a host country

. for acknowledging the land of Australia as the spiritual home of these traditional custodians

. for recognising the faith and spirituality of the Aboriginal Peoples of Australia

. and for pursuing a treaty process in good faith between the settlers, the land and the Aboriginal Peoples of Australia.

The formal ACKNOWLEDGEMENT is printed in Chapter Ten in a format suitable for independent distribution at events where groups are invited to endorse and publicly announce their support for the acknowledgement and pursue the treaty process.

I wish to thank Ivan Copley, one of my Aboriginal mentors, for his advice in the formulation of this Acknowledgement which, in its previous form, was designated a Sacred Apology and prepared as a sequel to the Apology made to the Aboriginal Peoples of Australia in 2008.

Ivan Copley recommends that those who accept the invitation to make a public Acknowledgement contact their local Reconciliation organisation (e.g. reconciliationSA@adam.com. au), or the National Congress of Australia's First People, PO Box 1446, Strawberry Hills, NSW, 2012.

CHAPTER ONE

The Primal Promise to Abraham

I begin my journey along the Abraham trail, aware of where I was fifty years ago and of the crucial significance today of the primal promise made to Abraham.

Fifty Years Ago and Since

Fifty years ago, in America, I wrote an article entitled *The Gospel Promise to Abraham*. In that article I wrote from the perspective of a conservative young Lutheran bent on celebrating the Gospel. I therefore read the primal promise to Abraham (Gen. 12:1-3) in line with St Paul's spiritual interpretation of the promise to Abraham as 'the Gospel preached beforehand to Abraham' (Gal. 3.8).

Fifty years ago I understood the promise to Abraham as a turning point in salvation history:

This moment is presented as a radical turning point in human history. Yahweh announces his plan of hope through Abraham. That announcement may be called the gospel for Abraham. Here is the news that has the power of bringing people back into a right relation with God (Habel 1969, p. 27).

Forty five years ago I returned from America—a promised land for pilgrims and early American settlers—to my home country of Australia that was also a promised land for many early settlers. At that time, I began to wonder about the promised land ideology and the implied identification of the indigenous peoples of these lands as uncivilised Canaanites. Were the Aboriginal Peoples of Australia equivalent to the peoples of Canaan who welcomed Abraham? Was Australia equivalent to the original land of promise?

Twenty years ago, I was the scribe for the Rainbow Spirit elders in Queensland. In the course of a workshop, with George Rosendale as our Aboriginal leader and elder, we also connected with the Abraham trail. According to these elders, when the missionaries spoke about the land, they often spoke about the promised land of Canaan where God led the chosen people of Israel. And Joshua was hailed as the great hero who conquered that land and supposedly fulfilled God's promise. In response, the Rainbow Spirit elders recognised that

> *Little was said (by the missionaries) about the indigenous people of the land whom the Israelites conquered. No questions were asked about whether Joshua's scorched Earth policy was what God really wanted for the indigenous people. Today Joshua's mode of operation sounds to us very much like that of the British colonial conquerors. Did the British have to follow Joshua's way?* (1997, p. 82).

The primal promise to Abraham, rather than the so-called fulfilment of the promise by Joshua, was the precedent the Rainbow Spirit elders endorsed and responded as follows:

. *Abraham, the peacemaker, respected the peoples of the land. We ask the same.*

. *Abraham recognised the God of the land. We ask the same.*

. *Abraham and the peoples of the land shared mutual blessings. We ask the same* (1997, p. 85).

I believe it is now time to honour the word of these elders, acknowledge their land and recognise their spirituality. To do just that, we return to the primal promise given to Abraham and trace its history.

The Primal Promise

The primal promise made to Abraham (in Genesis 12:1-3) has four basic components:

. the land of the promise

. the blessing of the promise

. the God of the promise

. the peoples of the land of the promise

At various stages along the trail I will analyse these four key components in the texts of Genesis. The task will be to retrieve: the initial land of the promise; the initial God of the promise; the initial the peoples of the land. By retrieval I mean identifying those underlying components of the text that probably belong to the original Abraham legend but have been modified by later Israelite narrators and redactors.

In my analysis I will also focus on the various ways the promise was interpreted and re-interpreted by biblical writers over the centuries to meet their changing agendas over the centuries. In short, my goal is to retrieve ancient markers along the trail, markers that are preserved in early traditions connected to the Abraham trail.

Truth Time

It is time for me,

as a biblical interpreter,

and a so-called contemporary Lutheran,

to discern not only that

the primal promise of Abraham is

a pivotal message in the Judeo-Christian tradition,

but also a stark reminder

of how we have ignored the basic connections

we have with the peoples of this land

and with the land itself.

Chapter Two

The Original Land of the Promise

Canaan is identified as the original land of the promise. Initially Canaan is portrayed as a host country whose indigenous inhabitants welcomed immigrants such as Abraham and helped them settle peacefully.

The Abraham Trail

The Abraham trail begins in a location identified as 'Ur of The Chaldeans'. Abraham's father, Terah, leaves his homeland, the land of his birth, and travels with Abraham, Lot and their wives to migrate to the land of Canaan. The land of Canaan is the apparent goal of their immigration plan from the beginning.

Why they leave the land of their ancestors to travel to the land of Canaan is not specified by the narrator. For some unknown reason, Canaan is the chosen location and the goal of their journey.

The journey of the family of Terah, including Abraham, may be compared with the journey of early immigrants to Australia and other colonies. Families came from many lands across Europe; the first settlers included Irish, British, Germans, Wends. They undertook long journeys to a distant land down under. Reasons for travelling to Australia included religious persecution, poverty due to potato rot and the dream of a better land.

My great grandfather left Prussia in the 1850s because he and his brother refused to be conscripted into the Prussian army to kill fellow human beings, many of whom were neighbours. For many of these immigrants, Australia was a land of promise for the future of their families. In a sense, they too followed the Abraham trail.

The family of Terah and Abraham interrupted their journey and settled in Haran about half way to the land of Canaan. Again, no reason is given as to why they 'settled' in Haran. The land of Canaan, however, seems to have been their ultimate destination.

Then we face the first dramatic moment on the trail of Abraham. After Terah dies, according to the narrator, Abraham hears a call to follow his father's impulse to make a complete break, leave his paternal world—country, kindred and house—and migrate to the land of Canaan. At this moment, the narrator introduces the 'primal promise' whose crucial components we will trace along the Abraham trail:

> *Then YHWH said to Abram, "Go from your country and your kindred and your father's house to the land that I will show you. And I will make of you a great nation, and I will bless you and make your name great, so that you will be a blessing. I will bless those that bless you and him who curses you I will curse and by you all families of the land will bless themselves* (Gen. 12:1-3).

We should already note at this point that this narrator—writing at a much later time—uses YHWH, the Israelite name for God, a name that was only later revealed to Moses (Exod. 6:3). We need to read this text in anticipation of later texts that reveal the actual name of the God that Abraham knew: El Elyon (see Chapter 3).

The Initial Land of Promise

When the extended Abraham family arrives in Canaan, they travel through the land to a place called Shechem. It is apparent, when we join the Canaanites who lived along the Abraham trail, that Abraham was made welcome. Abraham's extended family is not treated as a bunch of strange refugees or unwanted immigrants. Abraham was extended a welcome. Canaan was a welcoming host country as I indicated in my volume *The Land is Mine*:

Abraham passes 'through' the land, an act that can hardly be dismissed as innocent sightseeing. It is precisely at this point in the text (12:6) that the Canaanites, the indigenous inhabitants of the land are introduced. The land is not empty, but neither is it hostile. Abraham freely surveys a friendly territory, belonging to the host people of the land, where he or his descendants may stake a claim (Habel 1995, p. 108).

From the perspective of the Canaanites in this narrative, Abraham is a welcome immigrant who joins with the Canaanites at their sacred sites and becomes one of the community. The Aboriginal Canaanites and the Abraham family share the land of Canaan as common country. The initial Abraham trail is one of wandering and welcome in a land of promise for all 'the families in the land'.

Canaan was clearly a host country that welcomed the extended family of Abraham as active members of the local community.

The land of Canaan is presented as a host country inhabited by a range of peoples whose rights and culture Abraham respects. These rights include their rights to own, share, sell and negotiate the use of the land in the host country (Habel 1995, p. 132).

Canaan, however, is more than a host country where Abraham plans to settle. Time and again Abraham becomes aware of sacred sites where he experiences the Creator Spirit of Canaan. These sites include Salem, the Oak of Moreh, the oaks of Mamre, and the tamarisk of Beersheba. The land of Canaan is the new spiritual home of Abraham and his extended household. The Creator Spirit of Canaan makes them welcome in their new home at these sacred sites.

Australian Readings

How different is this experience to what happened in colonies like Australia when the European Christians, who revered the memory of Abraham, wandered through the land of the Australian Aboriginal Peoples. They regularly treated the local Aborigines as unwanted inhabitants, who were considered tantamount to savages. Their voice was ignored and their presence unwanted!

As early as the 1840s, the Australian Aboriginal Peoples were considered an impediment to settling the promised land.

> *They were considered part of the fauna and flora, like dingoes and emus—something to be cleared from the land to allow farming and grazing to develop in a safe, tidy and profitable environment* (Habel 1999, p. 81).

The suppression of the aboriginal Canaanite voice in the biblical tradition persisted in the development of European colonies throughout the 19th century and beyond.

If we now identify with the Canaanites in the Abraham narrative, the implications of this text, throughout the history of colonisation, are horrendous. The interpretation of this text by the Christian colonists has served as a basis for the violent destruction of rich spiritual cultures.

Unlike Abraham, most colonial settlers in Australia,

. did not develop positive relations with the families of the land

. did not recognise the sacred sites of the peoples of land

. did not make a treaty with the peoples of the land and recognise their rights and the rights of the land

The Aboriginal Peoples, understandably, would not be inclined to adopt the values of the invaders. As Lines writes,

> *They preferred independence of action, followed their own values and refused to adopt those of the invaders. They remained unconvinced—with the sight of men chained together in gangs, working under armed guard, floggings and public hangings—of the superiority of the invaders' civilisation (1991, p. 42).*

There were, however, a number of exceptions. Not all settlers came to Australia intent on replacing the inhabitants and possessing their land. My great-grandfather Wilhelm Habel, for example, came to Australia to escape being conscripted into the Prussian army in the middle of the 19th century. When he settled near Lake Linlithgow, he established a bond with Aboriginal elders and became familiar with their world even though his farm was on their land.

On one occasion, when British farmers ploughed up an Australian Aboriginal burial ground, they collected the skeletal remains as trophies and hung them up in their sheds. My great-grandfather was approached by a distraught Aboriginal elder and was appalled; he went from farm to farm, collected all the bones and collaborated with the Aboriginal elders to ensure the bodies were re-buried in such a way that the Aboriginal ancestors would finally be at peace. This example of ripping up Aboriginal burial grounds is, for me, equivalent to 'crucifying' sacred land (Habel 2013, p. 126).

Early South Australia

In early South Australia there were also moves to make a treaty with the Australian Aboriginal Peoples. Mark Brett has outlined this development in his article *A Suitably English Abraham*. In response to the South Australian Colonization Act of 1834, the Resident Commissioner in South Australia was instructed:

> *You will see that no lands which the natives may possess in occupation or enjoyment be offered for sale without previously ceded by the natives to yourself. You will furnish the protector of the Aborigines with evidence of the faithful fulfilment of the bargain or treaties which you may effect with the Aborigines for the cession of lands* (Brennan 2010 p.101).

As Brett notes, similar strictures preserving Aboriginal land rights were explicitly incorporated in the South Australian Amendment Act of 1838, but are missing in the Waste Lands Act of 1842 (Brett 2017, p. 111). The principles outlined in a submission by the Aboriginal Protection Society in 1840 reflect an early effort to protect the rights and sovereignty of the country as an independent nation, the right to exercise personal liberty and the right to protect the property and life for each individual of that nation (Brett 2017 p. 112).

In *The Land of Promise*, a very early history of South Australia published in 1839, John Stephens maintains,

> *"The native population" says the editor of the Southern Australian, "mingle fearlessly with our families and daily acts of kindness bind them to us. For the first time in the history of colonisation, the civilized and the uncivilized man have met without collision, and emigration has brought with it a blessing rather than a curse." At one of the recent meetings of the Aborigines' committee, the right of the natives to the soil had been discussed; and the obligation which their moral, if not legal claim to the land in the occupation of the colonists, imposed upon the settlers to use every means in their power for their benefit, was acknowledged (p. 222).*

The possibility of following the Abraham precedent and 'acknowledging' the rights of Aboriginal Peoples, persisted during those early years of South Australia, but, sad to say, the so-called promised land was soon viewed as a land of waste. *As history unfolded, the legal concept of 'the land of waste' was to prevail over the natural rights of Aboriginal people as economic interest relentlessly came to the fore* (Brett 2017, p. 118).

Truth Time

It is time,

not only to acknowledge

that our ancestors—unlike Abraham—

invaded the land of the Australian Aboriginal Peoples,

but also to recognise

that if they had been true to the original Abraham legend,

that this was a comparable land of promise,

they would have sought to settle peacefully

and cooperate with the custodians of the land

just as Abraham became a blessing

for all the families of the promised land.

CHAPTER THREE

The Original God of the Promise

The original God of the promise is El, the Creator Spirit of Canaan, who is worshipped by Abraham and the Canaanites.

An Invasion of the Land

There is a key moment along the original Abraham trail that has largely been forgotten or ignored. That moment is when we discover the name and nature of the God of Abraham preserved in an ancient liturgical blessing in Genesis 14:19 which reads:

Blessed be Abram by El Elyon,
Maker of sky and land.

The background to this blessing of Abraham by a Canaanite called Melchizedek, is an invasion of Canaan by an Eastern king, Chedorlaomer, and his allies who join forces near the Salt Sea. One goal of their invasion was to seize the minerals found in Sodom and Gemorrah. The kings of Sodom and Gemorrah fled to a mountain, but were captured. The invading kings also captured Lot, Abraham's nephew, who was living in Sodom at the time (Gen. 14:1-12).

One of the escapees who fled to the Oaks of Mamre was an Amorite, a friend and ally of Abraham. This reference reveals that, according to the Abraham legend, Abraham was not only welcomed by the local Canaanites; he formed important social ties with them—ties that became apparent in crises, such as the invasion by the Eastern king, Chedorlaomer.

When Abraham hears that Lot had been taken captive, he organises his 'trained men,' members of his extended household who had been born during his stay in Canaan.

Abraham's troupe consisted of 318 men. They were ready to fight for Abraham, who leads his would-be-soldiers to the North as far as Dan. Being few in number, Abraham decides to use strategy rather than brute force. He divides his men, attacks his enemy by night, manages to rout them and pursue them, quite a considerable distance: to the North of Damascus. Having defeated his foe, he redeems the goods taken from Sodom and brings them home along with Lot, the stolen women and the men who had also been captured.

The Blessing of El Elyon

Abraham's victory moves the King of Sodom to meet Abraham in the Valley of Shaveh and express his deep gratitude. Melchizedek, the King of Salem, not only comes out to greet Abraham; he also celebrates the occasion with bread and wine. This action indicates that Abraham has been welcomed into the host country by notable representatives. Abraham is now an integral part of the Canaanite community.

At precisely this point, the narrator informs the reader that Melchizedek is not simply one of the many kings of Canaan, like the King of Sodom. Melchizedek is identified as the high priest of El Elyon, often translated God, Most High. Abraham is welcomed into the host country by a Canaanite high priest, a tradition that a later Israelite narrator, rather ironically, preserves.

Melchizedek blesses Abraham using an ancient liturgical formula, frequently translated 'Blessed be Abram by El Elyon, Creator of Heaven and Earth'.

A close reading of this formula reveals that the god, El, is given the exalted name of Elyon—a title used a number of times in early liturgical texts referring to God as 'Most High' (Deut. 32:8; Ps. 87:5). El is a high god, who is exalted as Elyon both in the Old Testament and other related ancient texts.

El, the Creator Spirit

El, however, in this context is not simply another name for God. El, as the ancient Ugaritic Canaanite texts attest, is the Creator Spirit of Canaan. A detailed analysis of El as the Creator God of Canaan is provided in Marvin Pope's classic work: *El in the Ugaritic Texts* (1955). El is the Creator Spirit associated, first and foremost, with Earth and the land. As Pope states,

> *There is nothing in the Ugaritic texts to indicate that El was a celestial deity. All the evidence tends to connect El with earth* (Pope 1955, p. 52).

El is not only designated Elyon, however; El is also *qone shamayim w`arets*, a title whose translation has long been disputed. The verb *qana* most frequently means 'acquire' as in Proverbs 4:7: 'The beginning of Wisdom is this: acquire Wisdom.' *qana* may also mean 'beget' as it does in several Ugaritic texts and probably in Ps. 87:5. Most scholars now maintain that the verb means 'create' or 'form' as it probably does in Deut. 32:6 and in Ps. 139:13 where God 'forms' a human embryo in the womb of mother Earth. It is clear that this verb identifies El as the source of the diverse realms of Earth described in Genesis 14.

The realms identified as *shamayim wa'arets* are frequently rendered 'heaven and Earth', following the traditional rendering of that phrase in Genesis 1.1. A close examination of the formula, however, suggests a different rendering. It is clear from Genesis 1:6-8 that the 'firmament' that separates the waters is not heaven, the domain of heavenly beings, but sky or the skies. And the term usually rendered Earth is rendered 'land' throughout the Abraham narrative, whether that be a reference to the promised land or the land of some other people.

An alternate translation that reflects the age and context of this formula could well be,

'El, Elyon, the one who formed the sky and the land', or
'El Most High, maker of sky and land'.

El is the God of the land, the Creator Spirit who formed the land and who dwells in the land. El is the God of Canaan, the Creator Spirit worshipped at Salem.

Frank Moore Cross, in his detailed analysis of the Canaanite God El, concludes that 'It is patent that El is the creator God of the Canaanites and that *qone 'ars,* at any rate, applies exclusively to him' (1973, p. 51).

In one Canaanite text (The Ugaritic Keret text) El is repeatedly called 'The Kindly One, El, The Merciful.' El reveals his purpose for Keret in a dream and promises him progeny. The moral aspect of the character of El is seen in his directive for Keret to do no violence to a particular town (Gray, p. 119). El is the compassionate Creator God of Canaan. Pope describes the temperament of El as benevolent and sympathetic, with a title that could be rendered 'Beneficent El Benign' (pp. 44-45).

The blessing of Abraham includes an acclamation of El for delivering the invading enemies into Abraham's hands. The Creator God of the land of Canaan is here praised for employing Abraham, the new immigrant, to rescue the land from foreign predators. This formula suggests that Abraham has indeed been welcomed into the land by El, the God of the land, and therefore by the land itself.

Response to the Blessing of El

Abraham's initial response to the blessing by Melchizedek is to give El Elyon a tenth of everything he has taken as booty in battle (Gen. 14:20-24). This tithe indicates that Abraham also expresses his gratitude to El, the Creator God of Canaan. Abraham thereby indicates his sense of belonging to the Canaanite community of the host country—and to their deity.

The interchange between Abraham and the King of Sodom reflects a further indication that Abraham is now one of the community and not some immigrant who is willing to take advantage of his victory. The King of Sodom's offer for Abraham to keep all the goods gained in the conflict may seem an understandable expression of thanks for Abraham's remarkable achievement that enabled the King of Sodom to return to his kingdom. Abraham responds, however, by declaring that he will not take 'a thread or a sandal' that belongs to the King of Sodom. Abraham has no desire to be seen as having taken advantage of his neighbours.

Understandably, the men who fought beside Abraham as allies in the conflict are given the right to take their share of the booty. The men are identified as Aner, Eschol and Mamre the Amorite, among whose oaks Abraham was living with his extended family. Abraham is thereby respecting the rights of the people of the land where he is now a settler.

Abraham's response is preceded by an oath to 'El Elyon, Maker of Sky and Land', thereby confirming that Abraham is not only respecting the faith of his Canaanite community, but also making direct spiritual connection with this Creator Spirit in Canaan and in so doing affirming his faith in El Elyon.

At this point (Gen. 12:22), this narrator of the Abraham legend, who lived several centuries later, feels obliged to make the title appear more orthodox and correspond more closely to later Israelite theology. He therefore adds the title YHWH to the original name El Elyon. The title is missing, however, in the Greek translation of the text, a translation that probably retains the original version of this liturgical formula. After being blessed by El, the compassionate Creator Spirit of the land, Abraham is willing to take an oath in the name of that deity, thereby indicating his recognition of the Creator Spirit of Canaan.

El, the Creator Spirit of Canaan, is clearly the God of Abraham during his life in Canaan, a fact made explicit by the later revelation to Moses that 'I appeared to Abraham, to Isaac and to Jacob as El Shaddai, but by the name of YHWH I did not make myself known unto them' (Exod. 6:2-3).

The Godless Aboriginal Peoples

In general, the early settlers viewed most Aboriginal cultures as worthless and heathen. Aboriginal cultures were considered 'depraved' when compared with the 'civilised' cultures of the invading Europeans. Early anthropologists classified Aboriginal Peoples in Australia as tribal or primitive (Habel 1999, p. 20).

Going against the trend, Ted Strehlow, who during his youth lived among Aboriginal Peoples near Alice Springs and learned their language, writes,

> *As Professor Stanner has expressed it, the older anthropological writers who described the beliefs of the Aboriginal population were baffled to find among the Australian tribes a religion without God, without any creeds or church or priests, without any concern for 'sin' or sexual morals (in the European sense). Yet modern anthropologists are undoubtedly correct in stating that each Australian Aboriginal group religion is a 'living faith'* (1971, p. 4).

Most early European settlers in Australia, unlike Abraham, did not recognise the God of the land, or any Creator Spirit among the Australian Aboriginal Peoples. The Aboriginal Peoples were viewed as savages without a consciousness of God.

In the early years of settlement in South Australia, however, there was an effort to allocate land to the Kaurna people and to educate their children in the Christian culture. One of the first to learn the Kaurna language was Hermann Koeler (1837), a German who was concerned about the rough habits of many early settlers. He also came to the following conclusion about the Australian Aboriginal Peoples,

If this entire race occupies the lowest rung of the human race in both physical and intellectual aspects, then these South Australians in turn represent the lowest of them all (Muhlhausler, 2011, 11).

The missionaries Teichlmann and Schurmann, who arrived soon after Koeler, established a school for Aboriginal children and taught them in their own language, Kaurna. They disagreed with Koeler. Schurmann in particular recognised their intelligence and discerned the image of God in their bearing and behaviour (Lockwood 2011, p. 24). In 1939, Schurmann wrote, 'I am amazed that the natives have not sunk even further because of their constant association with the English rabble, rough and ungodly beyond comprehension (Lockwood 2011, p. 24).

It is significant, however, that even among most of the settlers and missionaries who sought to educate and integrate the local Aboriginal Peoples in the Adelaide area, there is no obvious record of them recognising the God or the spiritual world of these inhabitants. They, too, assumed that the Aboriginal Peoples were ultimately godless savages, even if they sought to civilise and convert them to Christianity.

For some, the local Aboriginal custodians in the land were indeed tantamount to the Indigenous Canaanites who lived in the promised land as remembered in late versions of the Abraham tradition. In his book *One Blood*, Harris recalls,

*Were the Aborigines, asked William Hull in 1846, degraded descendants of the nations driven out by divine command to the uttermost parts of the earth and islands of the seas? It was not simply that like 'the Hittites, the Jebusites and the **Aboriginal Canaanites**' that had been left to the natural consequences of the effects of not retaining the natural knowledge of God, but 'that of all peoples in that condition the Aborigines were judged to be on 'the lowest scale of degraded humanity' (Harris 1990, p. 30).*

Truth Time

It is time to accept

that the God of Abraham

was not named YHWH,

the later God of the Israelites,

but El, the Creator Spirit of the land

of the Canaanites

who were not godless savages.

It is time to acknowledge

that our European ancestors did not

respect the indigenous peoples of the land

and their Creator Spirit

the way that Abraham did.

CHAPTER FOUR

The Creator Spirit of the Aboriginal Peoples

El, the Creator Spirit of the Canaanites and the Creator Spirit of the Aboriginal Peoples are comparable forces in the faith of indigenous peoples.

When I returned to Australia in 1974, after 18 years in America, I was alarmed at how little I knew about the culture of the Aboriginal Peoples in my own country. At first I began to give talks asking the question: What was God doing in Australia before the Europeans came? That question has a precedent. In the USA, a bold young professor challenged the famous theme of the Lutheran Hour: *Bringing Christ to the Nations.* He claimed that Christ was already in these nations long before the European came.

I might have joked somewhat, at first, and suggested God was 'down under' waiting for Captain Cook and the British to arrive, or cuddling koalas and other unique marsupials he had created to play with in much the same way he once played with Leviathan (Ps. 104:26).

The Rainbow Spirit

The God of the Aboriginal Peoples is identified by the Rainbow Spirit elders, one among many Aboriginal communities, in the following quote:

The Creator Spirit is known to Aboriginal Australians by many names, including Yiirmbal, Biame, Rainbow Spirit, Wandjna and, in Christian times, Father God (1997, p. 31).

The myth of this Creator Spirit, active at the beginning of creation, reflects the imagery of the myth in Genesis One.

In the very beginning, the earth was formless and empty of life. The Creator Spirit in the form of the Rainbow

Spirit, shaped the land, its mountains, seas, rivers and trees (1997, p.29).

According to the Rainbow Spirit elders, The Creator Spirit is not a celestial high god, but 'has been and still is present within the land' (1997, p.30).

The Rainbow Sprit is not to be discerned as an almighty being residing in the heavens and controlling events on Earth. The Rainbow Spirit is the life-giving power of the Creator Spirit that fills the land with numerous life-forces and spiritual forces. The Creator Spirit causes these life-forces to emerge from the land and the waters as living beings in the form of plants, animals, fish and birds. The land is the primal domain of the Creator Spirit, the locus for the source of all life-forces and spiritual forces.

Significantly, Rainbow Spirit theology recognises that 'human beings are also created from the land by the Creator Spirit and eventually return to that Spirit, who is present in the land' (1997, p.33). This leads to a recognition of the ongoing relationship of the Australian Aboriginal Peoples to the land down under:

In the beginning the Creator Spirit entrusted different lands to different people. To Aboriginal Australians, the Spirit entrusted the land of Australia and its waters. The Creator Spirit is the true owner of the whole land and its waters (1997, p. 36).

After serious reflection about the presence of the Creator Spirit, the Rainbow Spirit elders declared that Rainbow Spirit theology assumes that God, the Creator Spirit, has been speaking through the culture of Aboriginal Peoples from the beginning (1997, p.11).

After reflecting on the Aboriginal experience of the presence of the Rainbow Spirit in my land, the land down under, I again began to wonder about the presence of the Creator Spirit in

Australia recognised by those who immigrated to Australia, including people like my great grandfather. Was their Creator God really any different from that of the Rainbow Spirit elders?

The Creator Spirit and the Land

Specific areas of the land are entrusted by the Creator Spirit to the care of specific groups of Aboriginal Peoples. These groups are the custodians of the land, its laws, its stories, its resources, its families, its ceremonies, and its sacred sites.

The Rainbow Spirit elders point to key texts in the Scriptures as evidence that the God of the Bible confirms their belief that they were given Australia to be the land for which they are to be responsible. They point especially to Acts 17:26-27 which reads,

> *From one ancestor he {God} made all nations to inhabit the whole Earth, and he allotted the times of their existence and the boundaries of the places where they would live, so that they could search for God and perhaps grope for him—though indeed he is not far from each of us.*

This text is biblical evidence to support the faith of the Rainbow Spirit elders that the land of Australia was allotted by the Creator Spirit to the Australian Aboriginal Peoples—not to the European invaders. That evidence supports their claim to be responsible to the Creator Spirit to sustain the land and its bounty. For them, the Creator Spirit is the true owner of the land and its waters.

The Spirit of the Land

When I wrote my work on *Reconciliation* back in 1999, I explored the various ways one can interpret the Spirit of the Land discerned by the Aboriginal Peoples, the Rainbow Spirit being one such manifestation.

Among many Aboriginal Peoples, the Spirit of the Land was experienced as a life-giving presence below the Earth who causes life-forces to emerge from land and sea. The Spirit of the land is the energising force present in sacred rites, sacred sites and sacred stories. When the sacred stories are told and the rites are performed at specified sacred sites, the power of this Spirit is activated (Habel 1999, p. 96).

The Aboriginal Peoples' experience of the Spirit of the Land is linked with plants, animals and human spirits in particular places. As Patrick Dodson says,

> *The land is a living place made up of sky, cloud, river, trees, the sand; and the Spirit has planted my spirit there is my own country—it is something—and yet it is not a thing—it is a living entity. It belongs to me. I belong to it. I rest in it. I come from there* (Dodson 1993, p. 20).

Aboriginal Peoples' experience of the Spirit present in land may be somewhat different from my understanding of the Spirit in Christian tradition. But my understanding is not grounds for rejecting the Aboriginal Peoples' experience as pagan or heretical.

The Christian image of the Spirit as a celestial force who intervenes on Earth as a divine being or spiritual presence may be part of my heritage. In an emerging Australian Earth spirituality, the experience of the Spirit as the Spirit of the Land deep within creation may be just as significant. A spiritual kinship between humans, animals and the Spirit of the Land may at first have seemed 'other' for me, but now leads me to a potential new understanding of the Spirit I already know (Habel 1999, p. 99).

After exploring the spirituality of Aboriginal Peoples and writing my volume on *Reconciliation*, I was ready to speak of a spiritual heritage that links me to this ancient land, a land where I was born. I too have a spiritual bond with this land. I can now affirm the Spirit of the Land as a distinctive manifestation of the Spirit in a land common to Aboriginal Peoples and non-Aboriginal Australians.

I can now confess that the Creator Spirit I know was experienced as the Spirit of the Land in Australia long before Europeans arrived. Australia was not a godless land any more than the culture of the Aboriginal Peoples was devoid of the Spirit. The Spirit of the Land was known in Australia long before Abraham and Sarah knew the Creator Spirit in the land of Canaan.

Truth Time

It is time to acknowledge

that Abraham's relationship with El,

the Creator Spirit in the land of Canaan,

provides grounds

for those who immigrated to Australia

to celebrate the Spirit of the Land

known to the Aboriginal Peoples of Australia

as a spiritual force deep in the land.

CHAPTER FIVE

Covenant Versions of the Promise

The primal promise made to Abraham is interpreted by the Israelite narrators both as a covenant made by YHWH in anticipation of the Mosaic covenant with Israel at Sinai and a covenant made with El Shaddai, the Creator Spirit of Canaan.

The Narrators of the Abraham Text

Who are the narrators of the Genesis version of the Abraham legend?

Certainly not eyewitnesses or scribes who lived at the time of Abraham! Each narrator of the Abraham trail in Genesis is clearly an Israelite who is an advocate of YHWH, the God of Israel, an Israelite who believes Canaan is the land promised by YHWH to the people of YHWH, an Israelite who believes the God of Israel selected Abraham to be the first human being to experience the real presence of Israel's God, YHWH. The religious experiences of all other peoples—such as the Canaanites—are ignored.

The narrators clearly live several hundred years after the time of Abraham, after the days of Moses when, according to tradition, the identification of the God YHWH was made known to the people of Israel. Most narrators seek to make Abraham a devotee of YHWH and repeatedly identify El, the God known to Abraham, as none other than YHWH. In so doing, the narrators re-write history from an Israelite perspective and ignore the rich Canaanite heritage that is still present, deep in the traditions behind the text.

It is probably accidental, and indeed fortunate, that several narrators preserved fragments of the Abraham legend that belong to the time of Abraham. These fragments I outlined in Chapter Three where I identified El as the Creator Spirit of Canaan.

The Abraham narrative as a whole, however, has been carefully revised to make it consistent with later Israelite faith and in tune which what I will now identify as the 'promised land ideology.'

The Promised Land Ideology

The promised land ideology, I would argue, is a closed worldview that understands that a given land is divinely promised to a particular chosen people and that the previous inhabitants of that land no longer have any right to live in the designated land.

The promised land ideology is first apparent in the Hebrew Bible in the way that the narrator revises the Abraham legend to make Canaan the land promised exclusively to Israel even during the lifetime of Abraham. The essentials of the promised land ideology according to the narrators are that

. the God who communicated with Abraham was YHWH, the God of Israel

. the promise of land for Abraham's progeny was made by YHWH

. the promise of land was made to Abraham at pivotal moments in his life, moments that are crucial in the promised land tradition

. the promise of land was a divine mandate for the subsequent conquest of the land of Canaan by the Israelites

. this promised land ideology is pivotal to Israel's covenant relationship with YHWH.

Repeatedly, through the Abraham narrative, the God who communicates with Abraham is identified as YHWH—even though by name YHWH was only revealed to Moses centuries later. In the revelation of the divine name to Moses, one narrator declares,

> *I am YHWH. I appeared to Abraham, Isaac and Jacob*
> *as El Shaddai, but by the name YHWH I did not make*
> *myself known to them* (Exod. 6.2-3).

As noted earlier, El is here recognised as the God of Abraham, and the Canaanite God of the land, who carries a number of titles such as Shaddai (Mighty, Exod. 6:2), Elyon (Most High, Gen. 14:19) and Olam (Eternal, Gen. 21:33). This narrator claims that El, the God of Canaan, and YHWH, the God of Israel, are in reality the same God—a claim that reflects the ideology that YHWH has been planning Israel's possession of the promised land since the days of Abraham.

All of the promises of land to Abraham in Genesis are ostensibly made by YHWH, from the initial promise in 12:1 to the promises in 12:7; 12:14; 15:18; 17:1 and 22:16. According to most of the narrators, YHWH, the God of Israel, is the deity behind the promise to grant all the land of Canaan to the descendants of Abraham who are understood to be none other than the chosen children of Israel, the descendants of Abraham.

The Promise of Blessing

As indicated above, the initial promise allegedly made by YHWH (Gen. 12:1-3) declares:

. the progeny of Abraham will be blessed and become a great nation in the land where Abraham migrates

. Abraham will experience the blessing of YHWH and earn a great name

. Abraham will mediate blessing to all 'families of the land'.

The way in which Abraham will become a great nation is not specified. The expectation that, in the process, his descendants with occupy the land of Israel, formerly known as Canaan, is made explicit a few verses later (Gen. 12:17). How the descendants will occupy the land is, at this point, not apparent.

The blessing of Abraham is presumably linked to the

expectation that he will have progeny who will remember his name as a great ancestor of the past; this reality is evident throughout the Hebrew and Christian Scriptures.

The promise that Abraham will mediate blessing is a positive expectation that seems to relate to the lifetime experiences of Abraham among the Canaanite families who welcomed Abraham and his extended family. Many translations render this promise as relating to 'families of the Earth', an interpretation that seems to be implied by St Paul when he argues that followers of Christ will have a faith like that of Abraham (Gal. 3:8). In the immediate context, however, the promise relates to the possibility that Abraham, and presumably his progeny, will have positive relationships in the land of promise that will eventuate in mutual blessing to the inhabitants of the land.

Abraham and his progeny are not only promised land; they are expected to mediate blessing to the 'families of the land', that is, to the Canaanites!

Sad to say, when Abraham's progeny—the children of Israel—returned to the land after their time in Egypt, a relationship of mutual blessing was not understood by interpreters in the book of Joshua to be part of the ideology of the promise. The promised land ideology erases the idea of a mutual and reciprocal blessing.

A Covenant Version of the Promise: Right to Possess

In Genesis 15, the promise of land is no longer a promise of future expectations. It is now a charter, a covenant sealed by a powerful religious experience. The charter commences with the formula 'I am YHWH who brought you out of the land of the Chaldeans, to give you this land to possess' (Gen. 15:7). This formula is clearly modelled on the common formula, 'I am YHWH who brought you out of the land of Egypt' (Exod. 20:2). By using this formula, the narrator identifies the migration of Abraham from Ur as the work of the same God who brought Israel out of Egypt. In this way, El, the God of the land, and YHWH, the God of the Exodus, are identified by the narrator as the same God, in spite of Abraham's prior relationship with El, the Creator Spirit of Canaan.

The promised land ideology of the Abraham narratives introduces a special covenant that includes an entitlement to the land that is irrevocable and unconditional. As I have indicated elsewhere,

> *The land treaty narrative presents Abraham, who presumably reflects the mood of the implied audience, as duly sceptical: "How do I know I will possess it?" (15:8). The treaty ritual and theophany which follow offer reassurance that entitlement to land does, in fact, rest in an unconditional charter from the time of Abraham* (Habel 1995, 124).

The rights of the existing inhabitants of the land are ignored in this charter. Many of the existing indigenous inhabitants of the land are carefully listed, but no indications are given as to how these inhabitants will fare when Abraham's progeny take possession. The listing of these inhabitants by a narrator who is writing after the conquest of Joshua would seem to imply that these indigenous peoples would need to be forcibly displaced for the 'great nation' of Abraham's descendants to take possession. The treaty with Abraham in Genesis 15 does not include a treaty for co-existence between the indigenous inhabitants and invading Israelites.

The key features of this Abraham covenant/charter can be summarised as follows: the charter

. confirms the promise of land as an unconditional gift

. is ratified by a traditional formula and ritual

. identifies those parties who are to be removed from the land

. constitutes a divine mandate.

While the land is promised personally to Abraham, he is given no mandate to pursue the fulfilment of the promise in the immediate future. Nor does he take any initiative to claim legal possession of the land. Unlike Joshua, it seems, Abraham is not bent on a holy war. Nevertheless, the divine mandate is recorded in Genesis 15 by the narrator to substantiate the claim of the progeny of Abraham to dispossess the indigenous peoples of Canaan, peoples who once welcomed Abraham.

Another Covenant Version of the Promise: Eternal Presence

In Genesis 17, we meet another narrator, identified by scholars as the Priestly Writer. According to this narrator, the God who makes the original covenant with Abraham, is not YHWH but El Shaddai, the Creator Spirit of Canaan. El Shaddai addresses Abraham with the following declaration,

> *I am El Shaddai, walk before me and be blameless. And I will make my covenant between you and me, and will multiply you exceedingly* (Gen. 17:2).

A condition of this covenant is that Abraham's name is changed from Abram (exalted father) to Abraham (father of a multitude). This covenant assumes that El Shaddai will be the God of Abraham's descendants forever in Canaan. Canaan is the land of promise and associated with the eternal presence of El Shaddai.

> *Behold my covenant is with you and you will become the father of a multitude of nations... And I will establish my covenant between me and you and your descendants after you through their generations for an everlasting covenant, to be God to you and your descendants after you. And I will give to you and your descendants after you, the land of Canaan, for an everlasting possession, and I will be their God* (Gen. 17:4, 7-8).

According to Mark Brett, in contrast to the idea of a single nation under the law of Moses reflected in the covenant with

Israel, this Abraham covenant is an international one; in this covenant blessings flow to 'a multitude of nations' and not just Israel (Brett 2013, p. 208).

In the context in which the covenant is embedded, however, the Israelite orientation of the narrator and the covenant become apparent. The narrator identifies El Shaddai as YHWH in the opening verses of the chapter and expects Abraham and all his descendants to be circumcised as a mark of their covenant identity (Gen. 17:9-14).

The primal promise made to Abraham was clearly linked to a covenant with El, the God of Canaan. The original covenant is a Canaanite covenant, transformed over time by various narrators into an Israelite covenant, linked to the Mosaic covenant and the possession of the 'promised' land. Or, as Brett argues, the redactors of Genesis 17 could envisage a great nation extending from the River of Egypt to the Euphrates, thereby bringing blessings to all peoples of Earth.

But the later redactors of Genesis could only find in Genesis 12:1-3 the promise of a 'great nation' confined to the triad of Abraham, Isaac and Jacob. As a result, the multinational vision of the El Shaddai covenant in Genesis 17 was assimilated to reflect the bias of later Yahwism (Brett 2018, p. 14).

The Australian Version

If we now compare this version of the promised land tradition with the world of the Aboriginal Peoples of Australia when European settlers invaded, we can readily discern that the Creator Spirit, known by various names among the Aboriginal Peoples, would not be promising that the British could invade and dispossess the lands of the Aboriginal Peoples of Australia.

The advent of the European settlers was accompanied by belief in a deity who belonged to a different world. They did not even recognise, as Abraham did, the Creator God of the land present among the Aboriginal Peoples of the land.

For the settlers from a distant world to view Australia as a promised land was to assume that the ideology of the narrator in the Abraham narrative could be appropriated, in spite of the time, context and essential differences embedded in the original promised land tradition in Genesis.

Being an Australian, I cannot ignore local analogies between the indigenous Canaanite traditions and Australian Aboriginal history, analogies that help me read the Abraham narrative from a Canaanite perspective with a measure of insight and empathy.

Nor can I can now ignore that the promised land ideology influenced settlers like many early Australians and other colonists—like the Boers in South Africa—who saw the land where they settled as their promised land. How did the indigenous peoples in these settled countries understand their lands before they were settled by immigrants? How would they view the divine promise of their land to a settler called Abraham immigrating from the East?

Twenty years ago, John Wilken wrote an article on 'The Biblical Promised Land and the Australian Aboriginal Peoples'. He quite accurately recognised that,

> *For Aboriginal readers of the Scriptures this (the possession of the land by Joshua) must be an unfortunate resemblance to their own experiences since 1788, when they were the existing inhabitants whose land was gradually taken by European settlers, much blood being shed in the process, especially on the Aboriginal side....It is understandable that they would see their own experiences as reflected in the fate of the Canaanites dispossessed by the invading Hebrews* (1997, p. 87).

Wilken's aim in his paper is to find a possible solution to this problem, the problem of Joshua fulfilling the divine promise of land by dispossessing and killing the Canaanites. Wilken's possible solution, grounded in his Christian spirituality, is tantamount to evading the reality of the situation—both in the Scriptures and in the experience of the Aboriginal Peoples of Australia. He concludes:

> *Christians can see the fulfilment of the land promise in the man Jesus of Nazareth, who grew up in Palestine and treasured the historical memories shared by all his people. In his risen life, he is related to all land and all people, fulfilling the promise to Abram that 'in you, all peoples of the earth will be blessed* (Gen. 12:3; cf. Acts 3:25; Gal. 3:8). (1997, p. 97)

I am well aware that the promised land tradition has been read and interpreted from a range of perspectives. In the Australian context, however, we dare not 'spiritualise' the promised land mandate of the Abraham trail. The initial invaders viewed Aboriginal Peoples as comparable to the Canaanites who had no right to the land and that being dispossessed was God's will. The memory and faith of Abraham, a friend of the Canaanite Aboriginal Peoples, is dismissed.

Truth Time

It is time to acknowledge

that the classic promised land ideology

seems to reflect

a bias

based on a belief that one chosen people

has a divine mandate

to invade and possess a particular land

and dispossess the indigenous inhabitants of that land

as peoples without rights,

peoples such as the Australian Aboriginal Peoples.

CHAPTER SIX

A Forgotten Treaty

The Land Treaty made between Abraham and the Canaanite Abimelech incorporates principles that may provide a precedent for a treaty in Australia.

A Canaanite Man of Honour

The story of Abimelech and Sarah (in Genesis 20) comes as something of a surprise as we follow the Abraham trail and discern the work of another narrator. When Abraham is moving around in Canaan, he comes to Gerar and meets Abimelech. Abraham says that Sarah is his sister and, as in an earlier episode, indicates, 'she is beautiful to behold' and therefore a desirable woman from Abimelech's perspective. This is not the aged Sarah who laughs at the possibility of sexual pleasure; this is a seductive Sarah from a much earlier time in her life.

There is every reason to believe Abimelech is a Canaanite who lived in the Negeb. Gerar is an independent Canaanite kingdom and the name Abimelech (the King is my Father) is a Canaanite name. The later reference to Abimelech as a Philistine (Gen. 26:2) is clearly an anachronism, since the Philistines did not invade this area until much later. Abraham is dealing with an honourable member of the local community, who has welcomed him.

When Abimelech takes Sarah to be his wife, the narrator reports that God came to him in a dream informing him that she is a man's wife. The account has clearly been 'corrected' by the later narrator who has identified this God as YHWH. Given the later reference to El Olam (Gen. 21:33), however, I would argue that we once again have an earlier legend in which the Canaanite God El is the deity in question.

Abimelech argues his case with this God who recognises Abimelech's integrity and convinces him to return Sarah to her husband Abraham or there will be serious consequences. Once again, we have a narrative that presents a Canaanite as a man of honour whose integrity is further demonstrated in the episodes that follow.

The Land Agreement

Abimelech, after informing his servants about the crisis, summons Abraham and challenges him honestly:

> *What have you done to us? And how have I sinned against you, that you have brought on me and my kingdom a great sin? You have done to me things that ought not be done!* (Gen. 20:9).

Abraham's response is

> *I did it because I thought there was no fear of God (Elohim) at all in this place and they will kill me because of my wife* (Gen. 20:11).

Abraham explains further that Sarah is indeed his half-sister and that she had agreed to say she is his sister rather than his wife wherever they wandered. It is striking that Abraham presumes there is no fear of God in the place, given his prior experiences with Melchizedek when he joined with Canaanites in the worship of El—assuming they were prior experiences.

The goodwill of Abimelech is immediately apparent. He offers Abraham, sheep, cattle and females slaves and returns Sarah his wife. What a generous gift! He even makes an agreement that Abraham could dwell wherever he pleased in Abimelech's territory. This land agreement is supplemented with a gift of a thousand pieces of silver as public evidence of his reconciliation with Abraham.

The episode concludes with Abraham praying to Elohim, which functions here as another name for El, who heals Sarah and Abimelech's family. The narrator, however, could not refrain from adding a postscript indicating that it was really YHWH, who has 'closed the wombs of all in the household of Abimelech'. YHWH is viewed as the God of retributive justice imposing a punishment that Abimelech clearly does not deserve. Abraham, on the other hand, goes unpunished.

From a Canaanite perspective, YHWH is here again portrayed as a biased deity—one with whom I would not readily associate.

The Land Covenant—Treaty

The Abimelech story continues after the birth of Isaac. Abimelech and the commander of his army come to Abraham with a specific request:

> *God is with you in all that you do;*
>
> *now therefore swear to me here by God,*
>
> *that you will not deal falsely with me or my offspring*
>
> *or with my posterity,*
>
> *but as I have dealt loyally with you ,*
>
> *you will deal with me*
>
> *and with the land where you have sojourned* (Gen. 21:22-23).

And Abraham swears that he will abide by Abimelech's request. Here we see a Canaanite taking the initiative and building a constructive relationship for the future. It is important to note that the agreement relates not only to the progeny of both parties, but also to the land itself.

This domain of Canaan is common property, not land promised to only one party!

The agreement is tested when a complaint arises about the well of water that the servants of Abimelech allegedly seized. Abimelech pleads ignorance and Abraham responds quite generously by offering Abimelech seven ewe lambs as a witness that Abraham has dug the well.

Once again Abraham and Abimelech swear an oath and make

a covenant, a treaty that is marked by a tamarisk tree planted at Beersheba. The oath, significantly, is sworn in the name of the Canaanite God El, here give the title Olam, Eternal One. The narrator, as we would expect, modifies the title by adding the name YHWH.

This land covenant in this narrative is significant. It preserves an ancient tradition that Abraham's relationship with people of Canaan included positive agreements or treaties that were designed to persist into the future. It also demonstrates that the covenants Abraham made with the people of Canaan were made in the name of El, the God of Canaan.

As I indicated earlier in my volume on land,

> *By swearing an oath with the inhabitants before a local deity whom both parties recognise (El Olam, 21:23), Abraham not only respects the people of Canaan, but does justice by the land to which he has migrated and affirms the rights of its owners* (1995, p. 129).

A Treaty Precedent

The covenant-treaty that Abraham and Abimelech make provides a precedent worth considering in terms of the treaty proposed by Australian Aboriginal leaders today.

. The Abraham treaty is made between two human parties: Abraham the immigrant/sojourner who wishes to settle in the land of Canaan and

. Abimelech the host/inhabitant of the land of Canaan.

. The treaty is accompanied by a public ritual involving an exchange of goods.

. Both parties swear an oath to seal the treaty.

. The treaty is remembered by virtue of its connection with a tamarisk tree that Abraham plants and calls on the name of El Olam, the Canaanite God, to witness the treaty.

How might we translate this covenant-treaty between Abraham and Abimelech into a treaty appropriate for Australia? Several features deserve consideration:

. The immigrant settler does not claim any right to possess the land but makes a treaty that enables him and his descendants to settle in the land.

. Sharing the land is attested by an oath with the God of the land, El Olam.

. Neither party assumes the right to dictate terms to the other party.

. The treaty incorporates a promise that the immigrant party will not only 'deal loyally' with the host party, but also with the land itself.

Truth Time

It is time to accept

that a treaty process recognising the rights

and culture of the Aboriginal Peoples of this land

is well overdue

and needs to be initiated immediately,

and that the Abraham treaty

provides a traditional precedent

that ought to help motivate us

to promote a fair and open treaty

that takes into account

past and future relations between both parties.

CHAPTER SEVEN

The Militant Version of the Promise

In Deuteronomy and Joshua, the initial promise is transformed to become the divine right to destroy the peoples of Canaan as cursed enemies.

Possessing the Good Land

Memories of the Abraham trail persist in the book of Deuteronomy. According to the narrator, Moses, while still in the wilderness, is reminded that the land of Canaan is the destination for God's people because that is the promised land, the land promised to 'your fathers, Abraham, Isaac and Jacob' (Deut. 1:6-8).

Throughout the book of Deuteronomy, the promised land ideology is developed progressively: from a land that is promised to a land that is to be possessed and dispossessed; all the laws enunciated in Deuteronomy are to be faithfully obeyed to guarantee possession. The Abraham trail becomes a militant trail for possession of the land of Canaan by the people of Israel.

The narrator recognises that the land the Israelites enter has

Great and goodly cities which you did not build, and houses full of all good things, which you did not fill, and cisterns hewn out, which you did not hew, and vineyards and olive trees which you did not plant, and when you eat and are full, then take heed lest you forget the Lord who brought you out of the land of Egypt, out of the house of bondage (Deut. 6:11-12).

There is no recognition, however, that the Canaanites have been the custodians who have created a land that is not only full of promise but ready for future settlers to enjoy. The

Israelites are to thank their God for bringing them to the land but not to thank the Canaanite custodians for making the land, a land of promise and plenty.

The narrator also describes Canaan as a 'good land':

> *A land of brooks of water, of fountains and springs, flowing forth in valleys and hills, a land of wheat and barley, of vines and fig trees and pomegranates, a land of olive trees and honey, a land in which you will eat bread without scarcity, in which you will lack nothing* (Deut. 8:7-9).

Once again, the promise and plenty of the land is not celebrated as the work of the Canaanite custodians. Rather it is emphasised so that the people of Israel

> *will remember that it is your God who gave you power to get wealth that he may confirm his covenant which he swore to your fathers, as at this day* (Deut. 8:18).

The narrator of Deuteronomy hears the God of Israel recalling the covenant he claims to have made with Abraham in Genesis 15 as an oath that guarantees Israel will one day possess the good land of Canaan—if the people are faithful to YHWH and never worship idols. The narrator also hears the God of Israel saying,

> *And you shall do what is right and good in the sight of the Lord, that it may be well with you and that you may go in and take possession of the good land which the Lord swore to give to your fathers by thrusting out all your enemies from before you, as the Lord has promised* (Deut. 6:18-19).

In this version, the custodians of Canaan are not only to be dispossessed; they are also to be viewed as 'enemies' who are to be forced out of their own land by divine decree. From the perspective of a Canaanite, this declaration is totally unjustified. This decree is not the way of Abraham—the one to whom the promise was first given. The original Abraham trail through the host country of Canaan has been forgotten; the history of Abraham has been re-written by the narrator of Deuteronomy.

Destroying the Custodians

The animosity against the Canaanites persists in Deuteronomy to a point where they are not only to be thrust out,

> *But when the Lord your God brings you into the land to take possession of it ... and when the Lord your God gives them (the Canaanites) over to you and you defeat them you must utterly destroy them and you shall make no covenant with them* (Deut. 7:1-2).

What happened on the Abraham trail outlined in Genesis is completely forgotten and reversed. Abraham made friends with the Canaanites and made a covenant with them. A covenant! A treaty! The promised land ideology of Deuteronomy no longer reflects the way, the faith and the integrity of Abraham and his bond with the Canaanites as custodians of the host country. The promise to settle and share has been turned into a divine right to defeat and destroy.

The Abraham trail has been virtually obliterated and the 'destruction trail' has begun.

According to the narrator, the God blazing the destruction trail into a land—not of custodians—but of mighty enemies is

> *He who goes over before you as a devouring fire is YHWH your God; he will destroy them and subdue them before you, so that you may drive them out, and make them perish quickly as YHWH promised* (Deut. 9:3-4).

Once again the vision of the possession of the promised land is heightened and the God of Israel becomes a 'devouring fire,' blazing the way for entry and dispossession. Once again the ethos of the original Abraham trail has been forgotten and his friends are transformed into frightening enemies.

The narrator reports a further message from the God of Israel that the Israelites are not to assume that they are destined to possess the promised land because of their righteousness.

It is because of the wickedness of these nations that YHWH your god is driving them out before you and so that he may confirm the word which he swore to your fathers, to Abraham, Isaac and Jacob (Deut. 9:5).

The peoples of the land are no longer enemies to be confronted and defeated; they are nations who are so wicked that the God of Israel feels compelled to expel them from their traditional land. The friends Abraham supported and defended on the Abraham trail are now viewed as the epitome of evil.

Moses and the Promise

Moses also had to deal with the unrighteous people of Israel who, because of their unfaithful ways, were threatened with destruction by YHWH during their wanderings in the wilderness. In the end Moses prostrates himself before his God forty days and forty nights and reminds his God of the promise made to Abraham as the basis upon which Moses could depend and assure the redemption of his people.

And I prayed to YHWH, 'O Lord God, destroy not thy people and thy heritage whom thou has redeemed through thy greatness, whom thou hast brought out of Egypt with a mighty hand. Remember thy servants Abraham, Isaac and Jacob' (Deut. 9:26).

For Moses, the promise sworn to Abraham was also the final ground upon which the people are urged to be bound by a covenant that they are indeed God's chosen people:

You stand this day all of you before YHWH your God … that you may enter into the sworn covenant of YHWH your God, which YHWH makes with you this day, that he may establish you this day as his people and that he may be your God, as he promised you, and as he swore to your fathers, Abraham, Isaac and Jacob (Deut. 29:10-14).

The basis upon which Israel was chosen to be YHWH's people, and on which YHWH is to be their God, is the promise made to Abraham. Here again the early traditions of the Abraham trail are ignored. In spite of Abraham's recognition of El Elyon as his God and the God of his Canaanite community, later tradition maintains that the God of Abraham was YHWH, the God who promised him a land and a future with many descendants.

When Moses reaches the borders of Canaan, the narrator records that God commanded Moses to ascend Mt Nebo and 'view the land of Canaan which I have given to the people for a possession' (Deut. 32:48-53).

Canaan is no longer designated as the future location where the descendants of Abraham may settle, but a 'possession', a term implying that the people of Israel have a legal right to the land, a right assigned to them by their God. The so-called promised land is no longer the land where Abraham's descendants may settle and live peacefully with the Canaanites as Abraham did.

Moses, because he had earlier broken faith with his God, will not be permitted to join the Israelites when they enter Canaan. Instead, he is expected to die on Mt Nebo after viewing the promised land from a distance. Before he dies, however, YHWH says to him,

> *This is the land which I swore to Abraham, to Isaac and to Jacob, 'I will give it to your descendants'. I will let you see it with your eyes, but you will not go over there* (Deut. 34:4).

Moses does not have the privilege of actually following the Abraham trail inside of Canaan. For him, the promise is the foundation of Israel being the chosen people and the grounds for anticipating the possession of Canaan by Joshua and his warriors.

The Joshua Version

The narrator of Joshua records that after Moses death, YHWH reiterates the militant promise made to Moses.

Moses my servant is dead; now therefore arise, go over this Jordan, you and all this people, into the land which I am giving to them, to the people of Israel. Every place that the sole of your foot will tread upon, I have given to you as I promised to Moses (Jos. 1:1-3).

When Joshua sends spies into the land, they meet up with Rahab the harlot who confesses—probably to save her neck when the Israelites invade—that 'YHWH has given you this land' (Jos. 2:9). When the spies return to Joshua, they are convinced that YHWH has indeed given the land into their hands and that the local inhabitants are afraid (Jos. 2:24).

When Joshua invades the land and attacks the city of Jericho, it is clear that no mercy is to be shown. There is no positive memory of Abraham's relationship with the families of the land. Instead, there is a destruction trail.

At the seventh time, when the priests had blown the trumpets, Joshua said to the people, "Shout, for the Lord has given you the city. And the city and all that is within it shall be devoted to YHWH for destruction (Jos. 6:16-17).

After numerous episodes of conquest and destruction, the book of Joshua closes with a summary of the Abraham trail that YHWH recounts to Joshua. One surprising feature of this summary is the admission that Abraham 'served other gods' beyond the Euphrates (Jos. 24:2). The text is silent, however, about the Canaanite God El that Abraham knew after he arrived in Canaan.

Joshua's speech closes with the people of Israel making another covenant; they agree to be obedient to YHWH, the God who gave them the land and was the warrior deity who enabled them to defeat the peoples of the land and gain possession of the land (Jos. 24).

Truth Time

It is time to acknowledge

that the biblical tradition

associated with Moses

which led to the transformation

of the peaceful promise of land to Abraham

into a militant promise to possess the land

should not negate

the prior positive tradition of the Abraham trail

in which Abraham makes friends

and a treaty with the Canaanites,

the Aboriginal Peoples of the land.

Chapter Eight

The Spiritual Version of the Promise

When we follow the Abraham trail into the New Testament we discover a radical re-reading of the original promise in spiritual terms.

The Forefather

The Gospels begin with a genealogy which links Jesus Christ with Abraham, the forefather of the people of Israel.

The book of the genealogy of Jesus Christ, the son of David, the son of Abraham (Mat. 1:1).

Abraham, however, is more than the forefather of the people of Israel: after three periods of fourteen generations, Jesus is identified as a true descendant of their famous forefather. In short, the Abraham trail is believed to lead specifically to Jesus.

The Spiritual Promise in St Paul

When St Paul walks the Abraham trail he focuses on the response of Abraham to the promise of God in Genesis 15:6;

Abraham believed YHWH and it was reckoned to him as righteousness!

In the immediate context, the promise of God was that Abraham would have a son and ultimately as many progeny as there were stars in the sky (Gen. 15:4-5). Even though his wife Sarah was old and apparently barren, Abraham is reported to have believed the promise of God that he would have a son and his progeny would live in Canaan, the land of promise.

St Paul is not interested in the role of Abraham as a friendly settler who is at peace with the peoples of Canaan, nor does he take into account that Abraham is a worshipper of the Canaanite Creator God, El. St Paul's interest is exclusively in the report of the narrator that Abraham 'believed'. For St Paul, that meant Abraham was a man of faith, not a man of works:

> *Thus Abraham "believed God and it was reckoned to him as righteousness". So you see that it is people of faith who are the sons of Abraham. And the scripture, foreseeing that God would justify the Gentiles by faith, **preached the Gospel to Abraham**, saying, "In you shall all the nations be blessed". So then, those who are people of faith are blessed with Abraham who had faith* (Gal. 3:6-9).

St Paul, however, not only identifies Abraham as a man who believed the promise of God that he would have a son, but also goes so far as to interpret the promise of blessing mediated through Abraham as the Gospel—the message of salvation for gentiles. Abraham is portrayed as a true 'disciple of Christ', long before Christ was born.

In Romans 4, St Paul explores the life of Abraham even further, wondering about the spiritual validity of the blessing mediated through the faith of Abraham:

> *Is the blessing pronounced only on the circumcised, or also on the uncircumcised? We say that faith was reckoned to Abraham as righteousness. How then was it reckoned to him? Was it before or after he had been circumcised? He received circumcision as a sign or seal of the righteousness which he had by faith while he was still uncircumcised. The purpose was to make him the father of all who believe without being circumcised and who thus have righteousness reckoned to them* (Rom. 4:9-11).

According to St Paul, Abraham becomes the spiritual father of all who believe the promise, a promise that is extended to include faith in him who raised Jesus from the dead. The promise of land is ignored and the promise of great progeny is believed to relate to all gentiles who believe the Gospel. The promise is interpreted as a spiritual blessing; it has nothing to do with the original land or the specific peoples of the land of promise.

According to Brett,

> *Paul's interpretation of the Old Testament covenants makes it clear that all Christian identity arises primarily from the Abraham covenant, which brings blessings to the nations ... The story of Joshua's conquest of Canaan under the authority of Mosaic Law is, in this respect, not our story, and we can argue that it was wrong for Christians to imagine that Joshua's conquest could be imitated in colonial history* (2013, p. 210).

The Spiritual Promise in Hebrews

The writer of the book of Hebrews takes another step. This narrator interprets the faith of Abraham as a response to a call from God to leave his homeland and go where he would receive an inheritance and journey to an unknown land. The writer claims that Abraham

> *By faith sojourned in the land of promise as in a foreign land, living in tents with Isaac and Jacob, heirs with him of the same promise* (Heb. 11:9).

In Hebrews, faith seems to be the factor that determines every aspect of life on the Abraham trail. Abraham is portrayed as a model believer for Christians of the early church. The Abraham trail changes: from being the journey of a friendly settler who becomes an integral part of the Canaanite society to a stranger sojourning in a foreign land because of a call from a God who preached the Gospel long before the advent of Jesus Christ.

Earlier, the writer to the Hebrews interprets the figure of Melchizedek—the priest with whom Abraham worshipped El, the Canaanite Creator Spirit—in a spiritual mode. He says of Melchizedek that

> *He is without father or mother or genealogy, and has neither beginning of days nor end of life, but resembling the Son of God, he continues a priest forever* (Heb. 7:3).

Jesus is then identified as a 'priest forever after the order of Melchizedek,' who brings salvation to all who believe. In short, Jesus Christ is not only viewed as the biological descendant of Abraham but also the spiritual fulfilment of the original promise to Abraham. Melchizedek is understood to be Jesus' first coming in human form.

The First Missionary

St Paul's spiritual interpretation of the primal promise to Abraham has persisted as a Christian tradition until today—as my article from fifty years ago, mentioned in Chapter One, testifies.

There are, however, recent writers who have identified Abraham as the first missionary. A *Google* search for 'Abraham as First Missionary' discloses hundreds of articles and references that reflect a spiritual reading of the original promise to Abraham.

According to this current spiritual interpretation, Abraham became the first missionary to a foreign country because he left his homeland at the request of God. Through his call to leave his native land, God promised that through him a knowledge of salvation—justification by faith—would come to all nations.

Abraham becomes the forerunner of all modern missionaries, Canaan becomes a foreign land in need of salvation; the true progeny of Abraham are all who believe the Gospel.

Truth Time

It is time

to return to the original promise to Abraham,

and acknowledge that Canaan

was a host country that welcomed Abraham,

and that Abraham's spiritual experience

was not the Christian Gospel

but a rich life in a land of promise

with the God of that land,

El, the Creator Spirit of Canaan.

CHAPTER NINE

Promised Land or Crucified Land

The land of Australia was not a Promised Land but a Crucified Land for many Australian Aboriginal Peoples.

The Weeping Daughter

The image of Australia invaded and tragically abused is common among poets of the Aboriginal Peoples of Australia. In one of the most poignant of these images, the land as mother was crucified like the Only Son.

> *My mother, my mother*
> *what have they done?*
>
> *Crucified you*
> *like the Only Son.*
>
> *Murder committed*
> *by mortal hand.*
>
> *I weep, my mother,*
> *my mother, the land.*

Mary Duroux (1992)

The image of a crucified mother and her weeping daughter, Mary, evokes an empathy within me that I can no longer ignore. For Mary Duroux and many of her Aboriginal friends, Australia was anything but the promised land. For them, Australia had become the crucified land.

The wrongs and disasters inflicted on the Aboriginal Peoples have now been recognised by many empathetic Australians. Apologies have been made for many of the atrocities, such as abuses experienced by the Stolen Generations. Rites of healing and reconciliation with the Aboriginal Peoples have taken place across the country. My 'Rites of Healing at Seven

Sites' has been 'celebrated' in many places (Habel 1999, pp. 164-188).

The full implications of the evils perpetrated on the Aboriginal Peoples, their land and their spiritual world has, I feel, not been recognised publicly. The pain of the crucified land has reached deep—and the mother is still weeping.

The depth of the pain and the weeping is, to some extent, reflected in the memories of the Rainbow Spirit Elders. As they say,

> *The Creator Spirit is crying because the blood of the Aboriginal people has desecrated the land. The land is crying because the bloodshed on the land has not been heard, and the sacrifice of those who died has not been remembered. The people are crying because the crimes committed against their ancestors have not been revealed and appropriately recognised* (1997, p. 48).

And again,

> *The Creator Spirit is crying because the land is dispossessed.*
>
> *The land is crying, because the people assigned by the Creator Spirit to be its custodians have been torn from the land by force.*
>
> *The people are crying because they are unable to fulfil their responsibilities as custodians of the land* (1997, p. 45).

As this chapter in the book *Rainbow Spirit Theology* makes abundantly clear, the weeping is a spiritual as well as an emotional response to the trauma experienced as a result of the desecration and dispossession of the so-called promised land of Australia.

Accordingly, the response of Australian settlers ought to be more than a formal political apology. We need to come to terms with the spiritual abuse that has been part of our heritage. It is time for a sacred confession or at least a public *Acknowledgement* of the truth.

A Land Alive

For traditional Aboriginal Peoples, life-forces are present within the land and emerge at the impulse of the Creator Spirit. As custodians of the land, they perform rites at sacred places, thereby cooperating with the Creator Spirit in replenishing the land.

As the Rainbow Spirit Elders make clear,

> *In each Aboriginal person there is land and spirit. Both of these link each one of us with the land and the Creator Spirit in the land. For us Aboriginal people to know our true identity, it is vital for us to know the specific place in the land to which we belong* (1997. p. 38).

> *Aboriginal people know from the Creator Spirit, and from the land itself, that we are responsible for sustaining the land of Australia. The land from which we came, where our afterbirth is buried, is given us in trust. To breach that trust is to violate the law of the Creator Spirit, written in and on the land* (1997. p. 36).

For the Aboriginal Peoples, therefore, the land is not simply lifeless property to be possessed or dispossessed, to be cleared or cultivated, but rather a domain that is an integral part of their identity and of their spiritual world. In a sense, they are one with the land. And the land is alive, to be treated as a mother.

As George Rosendale, my Aboriginal mentor, once said to me, 'Inside me is spirit and land, both given to me by the Creator Spirit. There is a piece of land in me, and it keeps drawing me back like a magnet to the land from which I came. Because the land, too, is spiritual.'

The land that the Europeans invaded, settled, cleared and cultivated was more than property available to be possessed and exploited. The land was an integral part of the very identity of the indigenous peoples of the land. For them, the land was and is alive, permeated with life-forces, linked to their very being and animated by the Creator Spirit.

To desecrate this land and violate the peoples who were one with this land is, I believe, from their perspective, equivalent to 'crucifying' this land.

The Painful Nails

The numerous acts of desecration of the land, and the crimes committed against the peoples of the land, might be compared to the painful insertion of nails in the act of crucifixion. The following nails are among the many inflicted on the Aboriginal Peoples and the so-called promised land of Australia:

. the massacre of Aboriginal groups by official government parties

. the hunting down of Aboriginal Peoples like wild animals

. the poisoning of water holes and streams

. the desecration of sacred sites and Dreaming places

. the humiliation of Aboriginal human beings as being sub-human

. the vilification of Aboriginal spiritual life as evil and barbaric

. the removal of Aboriginal Peoples from the land that was their mother

. the wounding of the land by clearing, mining and polluting.

One of the most painful wounds inflicted on the land was the Black War in Tasmania; in the spring of 1830, an offensive was planned not only to dispossess but also to destroy the Aboriginal population of the state. A regiment of soldiers, police, prisoners and settlers formed a human chain across the settled districts of Tasmania. This human chain, known as the 'black line', moved relentlessly southward for three weeks killing every Aboriginal person they found.

Those who eluded the net were persuaded by a devious diplomat to surrender. Fewer than 200 indigenous Tasmanian survived; all of the survivors were wounded. When the remnants of these Tasmanian Aboriginal Peoples were exiled to Finders Island in Bass Strait, the land, it was claimed, had been cleared of natives.

As a result the land too suffered; its custodians and kin had been rent from their spiritual home and mercilessly slaughtered. In the eyes of the 'black war' soldiers, this killing may have been akin to the 'holy war' of Joshua, but from the perspective of any empathetic Australian, this was genocide of the people, and crucifixion of the land.

Another of these painful nails was the poisoning of waterholes to destroy those Aboriginal Peoples, like the Wiradjuri, who sought to keep their traditional lands.

> *At Poisoned Waterholes Creek near Ganmain, bags of flour were laced with arsenic and the water poisoned. A large party of more than 100 Wiradjuri arrived to camp, and within hours men, women and children were writhing in agony. Armed and mounted men then swept down on the camp from all sides, firing until the dead choking in the creek* (Grassby & Hill 1988, p. 44).

It is hard to believe that more than a hundred years after the poisoning of waterholes, the Australian government endorsed the poisoning of lands, life and sacred sites by exploding nuclear weapons in the centre of Australia. Lands like Maralinga and Emu were contaminated with radio-active poisons.

Aborigines at Wallatinna reported a 'big black mist' coming from the direction of Emu. This black radio-active cloud brought sickness and death to the people. The 'red' sands in the area, of which the people were proud, became 'poisoned' and turned grey. And this desecration of land and dehumanisation of Aboriginal Peoples was, according to the Australian government, for the 'greater good', by 'making historic advances in harnessing the forces of nature' (Habel 1999, 60-61).

The 'Cry of Mudrooroo' not only reflects the agony felt by

the abuse of the land but also the indictment of the Christian
church for its role in 'raping' the Earth:

Did Wandjina mark out this land,
Did he, did they—tell me?
Did Wandjina mark out this land,
Did he, did they? Yes, he did!
Well, what is this Christian God,
Teaching us to rape the earth,
Separate ourselves and rape the earth,
Lose our manhood as we rip our mother?
Did Wandjina mark out this land,
Did they, what is this denomination then?
This conquering, this power, this individuality?
Did Wandjina mark out this earth?
Who changed it, who changed it?
Was it this Christian God?
Was it this denomination of puny humans?
When they die, to whom do they return?
When they die, how will they face Wandjina who marked
out this land?
Didn't they, didn't he?—he did! (Mudrooro 1986, p. 10).

The first colony formed in South Australia was supposed to
be radically different from the convict colonies in New South
Wales and Tasmania. The settlers dreamed of a land that
would be a 'model colony', a promised land based on the ideals
of Edward Gibbon Wakefield. The expectation was that their
hard work of civilising the land would receive the blessing of
their God. The first two governors, Hindmarsh and Gawler,
were also interested in the welfare of the Aboriginal Peoples,
and the careful distribution of land suitable for agriculture
(Gibbs 1969, ch.3).

As indicated in Chapter 2, there were, in early South Australia, also moves to make a treaty with the Aboriginal Peoples. Mark Brett has outlined the development of these moves in his article *A Suitably English Abraham* (2013).

Sad to say, the high ideals of Wakefield and others were not realised. The Aboriginal Peoples eventually lost all their lands, and their sacred sites in the city became pubs, brothels and churches. Even the land of South Australia was 'crucified'.

Truth Time

It is time to acknowledge

that the Promised Land

became a Crucified Land,

that not only the Aboriginal Peoples

in Australia

suffered at the hand of European invaders,

but also that the land itself,

the mother whom the Aboriginal Peoples

nurtured

for thousands of years,

also suffered.

CHAPTER TEN

Acknowledgement

With an acute consciousness of our settlement history, after following the trail of an ancient settler called Abraham, we settlers acknowledge publicly,

in relation to land,

. that we have often discounted the capacity of Aboriginal Peoples to be custodians of the host country, **unlike Abraham** who recognised Canaan as the host country and settled in Canaan as a worshipping member of the community

. that the Aboriginal Peoples have been **custodians of this land** for thousands of years and have the right to claim continuing recognition for their role as custodians

. that the Aboriginal Peoples have the capacity, as custodians, to **read the landscape** and discern laws relevant for the welfare of the land

. that the Aboriginal Peoples have a **right to exercise sovereignty** over their lands and shape the future of the land

in relation to faith,

. that we have often dismissed Aboriginal beliefs in a Creator Spirit as paganism, **unlike Abraham** who recognised El, the Creator Spirit of the Indigenous Peoples of Canaan.

. that the Aboriginal Peoples have a dynamic **faith is a Creator Spirit** who transformed the landscape and who is actively present in country

. that Aboriginal faith and practice, reflecting a **rich spiritual awareness,** make a powerful contribution to the multi-faith culture of the land

. that for Aboriginal custodians **the land is alive**, replete with both life-forces and spiritual forces that ought to be respected

in relation to treaty,

. *that we have often ignored the capacity of Aboriginal Peoples to function as citizens of the host country and negotiate a treaty with the settlers, **unlike Abraham** who made a treaty with an indigenous community in Canaan, declaring loyalty, making a bond with the land itself and swearing by the Canaanite Creator Spirit*

. that, in the light of this *Acknowledgement* and *The Uluru Statement of the Heart,* we endorse a **treaty process**

. that a treaty process will publicly acknowledge **the identity** of the Aboriginal Peoples as the traditional custodians of the land of Australia, an identity that ought to be an integral part of the constitution of Australia

. a treaty process will publicly acknowledge **the voices** of the Aboriginal Peoples in the government of this country at a national and local level

. a treaty process will publicly acknowledge **the rights and laws** of the Aboriginal Peoples as the traditional custodians of the land and negotiate ways of incorporating these rights and laws into our Australian society to further the ecological welfare of the country and foster peace in our land

. a treaty process will publicly acknowledge **the sovereignties** of the Aboriginal Peoples, sovereignties that bind them spiritually to the land

. a treaty process will publicly acknowledge the **sacred nature of the land** and sacred sites in the land and negotiate ways to have their sacred status restored and celebrated

. a treaty process will publicly acknowledge the many forms of **spirituality** of the Aboriginal Peoples of this land and will agree to celebrate their faith, respect their sacred rites and affirm their beliefs as important contributions to the culture of this country.

CHAPTER ELEVEN

A Challenge for the Churches
to Recognise the Acknowledgement

The Missionary God

When I began listening to the voice of Aboriginal elders, especially the voice of my mentor, George Rosendale, I discovered that the God down under experienced by the Aboriginal Peoples was dismissed by most missionaries and 'white Europeans' as pure animism or trite paganism. According to the Rainbow Spirit elders,

> *One or two missionaries tried to understand our religion. For the most part, our religious beliefs and ceremonies were regarded as pagan, barbaric and evil* (1997, p. 2).

One of the elders confessed,

> *Jesus was thrust down my throat. I was not encouraged to think for myself or allow a theology to grow from within me as an Aboriginal. I was told what to do, what to think, where to live. I was not free* (1997, p. 4).

The missionary God was a traditional Triune God whom most missionaries believed had sent them on a mission to 'save souls', the pagan souls of Aboriginal Peoples. There was rarely any attempt to discover the Aboriginal God, or to understand how Aboriginal Peoples had experienced a Creator Spirit for several millennia. The spiritual relationship of the Aboriginal Peoples with the land was ignored.

A Challenge for Churches

Already back in the 19th century, my great grandfather held a mission festival on the banks of Lake Kennedy in Victoria. Lutherans would gather on the grass and the preacher would stand tall on a wagon and summon members to support the mission of the church.

Their support enabled missionaries—who were also linguists—to travel from Germany to bring the message of the Christian Gospel to Aboriginal Peoples in various locations, especially the Finke River in Central Australia. Missionaries from other denominations also established mission stations across Australia.

The many stories—both positive and negative—about what happened at these stations are not the reason for this sacred acknowledgement. My concern is how the churches of today, and other religious bodies, relate anew to the Aboriginal Peoples of Australia not only in terms of land rights and reconciliation, but also in terms of acknowledging that the spiritual tradition of the Aboriginal Peoples is not in conflict with our early Christian heritage—a tradition reaching all the way back to the relationship between Abraham and the Canaanites described in Genesis.

Are the churches of today ready to endorse the *Acknowledgement* outlined above and to confess that they have dismissed the spirituality of the Aboriginal Peoples when they ought to affirm not only its essence but also its continuity with the primal faith of our ancestor, Abraham?

The churches are challenged, by the ancient voices of Abraham and Sarah, to endorse this acknowledgement, make a declaration of common primal faith, and jointly plan

. *a rich celebration of the creative presence and spiritual pulse of the Creator Spirit throughout this country*

. *a new exploration of this country as an amazing source of profound spiritual wonders, mysteries and memories*

. *a willingness to read the Book of Nature with the Aboriginal Peoples as a source of revelation parallel with that found in the Bible*

. *a readiness to incorporate the insights, practice and memories of Aboriginal Peoples bonding with the land into our current evolving local and cosmic ecological awareness*

. *an agreement to return to the time when Europeans first entered into this land and invite our hosts, the Aboriginal Peoples, to welcome us into the land and make a treaty embracing the Creator Spirit, the host people, the settlers, and the land.*

It needs to be noted that there is currently a move by the Mennonite Church of Canada and other religious leaders to respect the spirituality of Aboriginal Peoples of Canada, and to develop a school curriculum that incorporates Aboriginal spirituality. A recent 2017 book entitled *Quest for Respect: The Church and Indigenous Spirituality* promoting this move has been published by the Mennonite Church of Canada.

Why is there no comparable movement in Australia?

A Second Challenge for Churches

In the year 2000, the Lutheran Church of Australia in its *Statement on Reconciliation* assured the Aboriginal Peoples of 'our continued support in working for you … for justice'. If the Lutheran Church, like other churches, is true to its word, then the Church should now be ready to announce publicly its support for an Australian treaty process as enunciated above.

In *We're All People*, the issues of racism, reconciliation and land rights were discussed in detail and the numerous recommendations indicated a commitment of the Lutheran Church to pursue justice for Aboriginal Peoples, including its 'support for the principle of land rights for Aboriginal people' (1997, p. 24).

The Lutheran Church, like other churches, has long recognised that—already in *The Letters Patent* of 1836—nothing in the founding of the colony was to take away the rights of Aboriginal Peoples, including their right to their lands. In 1939, Pastor Kavel wrote to the Colonial Commissioners calling for land to be set aside for the Aboriginal Peoples of South Australia.

Early Lutheran clergy like pastors Klose and Meyer advocated the establishment of property rights and boundaries for the Aboriginal Peoples.

In the course of history, however, those rights were ignored and the voice of early advocates of such rights seem to have been forgotten. In 2009, South Australian Aboriginal elders George Trevorrow, Thomas Trevorrow and Matthew Rigney, said,

We need to understand why our rights have been ignored when they were protected by King William IV... It makes no sense to us why our native rights to our lands and waters were protected in the Letters Patent but not in reality. We need to find answers to these questions for ourselves and our brothers and sisters from other Aboriginal communities in South Australia and across Australia (Berg 2010, Preface).

A Lutheran paper on 'Land, Justice and Lutheran Settlement in Australia' states:

*The Letters Patent of King William IV and the foundational documents of South Australia point us to the stark reality that our nation still has not addressed the issue of a fair and just settlement for Aboriginal peoples who were dispossessed of their lands. A Church that proclaims God's Grace and God's concern for justice may wish to join those calling on the Federal Government **to finally look at the issue of a treaty*** (1997, p. 4).

Yes, the time has come for the churches 'to finally look at the issue of a treaty.' The precedent of our forefather Abraham offers both a biblical motivation and a cultural exemplar for churches to move beyond past expressions of reconciliation. We need to confront the Australian Government with the need for a treaty that takes into account the injustices of the past and the denigration of the culture of the Aboriginal Peoples.

Truth Time

It is time

for the Christian churches in Australia

to acknowledge publicly

that frequently in the past

we have dismissed

the spirituality of the Aboriginal Peoples

as worthless animism,

and to confess that we share

a primal faith

with Abraham and Sarah,

and our indigenous friends,

whether in Canaan or Australia

or another colonial country

AND

to publicly declare our commitment

to help negotiate an Australian treaty

in tune with

the Uluru Statement from the Heart.

CHAPTER TWELVE

Conclusion

Yes!

IT IS TIME!

In the light of the faith of Abraham,
the positive relationships between Abraham
and the indigenous custodians of Canaan,
including worship of El, the Creator Spirit of Canaan,
a covenant with the same Canaanite God,
a treaty in which this God, Abraham, the Canaanites
and the land of Canaan are partners,

AND

in the light of how Australian settlers,
influenced by a promised land ideology,
dispossessed the indigenous custodians,
discounted their creation spirituality
and violated the land they held sacred,

IT IS TIME

for Christian churches
and the descendants of Christian settlers
to follow the precedent of Abraham,
to make a public acknowledgement,
a colonial confession,

AND

to promote a treaty process
that guarantees and respects the identity, rights,
sovereignty, country and spirituality
of the Aboriginal Peoples.

Bibliography

Berg, Shaun (ed.) 2010. *Coming to Terms: Aboriginal Title in South Australia* (Adelaide: Wakefield Press).

Brennan, Sean (2010). "The Disregard for Legal Protection of Aboriginal Land Rights in Early South Australia", in S. Berg (ed.) *Coming to Terms: Aboriginal Title in South Australia* (Adelaide: Wakefield), 90-121.

Brett, Mark (2013). 'Permutations of Sovereignty in the Priestly Tradition', *Vetus Testamentum* 63, 383-393.

Brett, Mark and Graham Paulson (2013). "Five Smooth Stones: Reading the Bible through Aboriginal Eyes", *Colloquium* 45, 199-214.

Brett, Mark (2017). 'A Suitably English Abraham: Emigration to Australia in the Nineteenth Century', in J. Havea (ed.), *Postcolonial Voices from Down Under: Indigenous Matters, Confronting Readings* (Eugene: Pickwick), 110-121.

Brett, Mark (2018). 'YHWH among the Nations. The Politics of the Divine Names in Genesis 15 and 14' in Jacob Wohrle and Mark Brett (ed.), *The Politics of the Ancestors: Exegetical and Historical Perspectives on Genesis 12-36* (Tubingen: Mohr Siebeck).

Cross, Frank Moore (1973). *Canaanite Myths and Hebrew Epic* (Cambridge: Harvard University Press).

Dodson, Patrick (1973). 'The Land our Mother'. *CCJP Occasional Paper, No. 9* (Melbourne: Collins Dove).

Duroux, Mary (1992). *Dirge for Hidden Art* (Moruya: Heritage Publishing).

Fretheim, Terence (2007). 'The binding of Isaac and abuse of children' *Lutheran Theological Journal*, 41, 84-92.

Friesen, Geoff & Steve Heinrichs (2017). *Quest for Respect: The Church and Indigenous Spirituality* (Ottawa: Mennonite Church of Canada).

Gibbs, R M (1969). *A History of South Australia* (Port Pirie: Balara Books).

Grassby, A & Hill, M (1988). *Six Australian Battlefields* (Sydney: Allen and Unwin).

Gray, John (1957). *The Legacy of Canaan* (Brill: Leiden).

Fretheim, Terence (2007). *Abraham: Trials of Family and Faith* (Columbia: University of South Carolina Press).

Habel, Norman (1964). *Yahweh versus Baal: A Conflict of Religious Cultures* (New York: Bookman).
- - (1971). *Literary Criticism of the Old Testament* (Minneapolis: Fortress).
- - (1969). 'The Gospel Promise to Abraham', *Concordia Theological Monthly*, Vol. XL, pp. 26-35.
- - (1991). 'Conquest and Dispossession: Joshua, Justice and Land Rights,' in *Pacifica* 4, 76-92.
- - (1995). *The Land is Mine. Six Biblical Land Ideologies* (Minneapolis: Fortress).
- - (1996). 'The Crucified Land: Towards our Reconciliation with Earth' in *Colloquium* 28/2, 3-18.
- - (1999). *Reconciliation. Searching for Australia's Soul* (Preston: Mosaic Press).
- - (2013). *The Tree Whisperer. The Story of Wilhelm Habel* (Reservoir: Morning Star).
- - (2018). *Why on Earth do you still wonder about God? Dancing with Doubt* (Reservoir: Morning Star).

Harris, J (1990). *One Blood. 200 Years of Aboriginal Encounter with Christianity: A Story of Hope* (Sutherland: Albatross).

Lemche, Niels (1991). *The Canaanites and their Land. The Tradition of the Canaanites* (Sheffield: Sheffield Press).

Lines, William (1991). *Taming the Great South Land. A History of the Conquest of Nature in Australia* (Sydney: Allen and Unwin).

Lockwood, Christine (2011). 'A Vision Frustrated: Lutheran Missionaries to the Aborigines of South Australia', in *Germans: Travellers, Settlers and their Descendants in South Australia* edited by Peter Monteath (Adelaide: Wakefield Press, 2011), pp. 17-40.

Loubser, Bobby (1987). *The Apartheid Bible. A Critical Review of Racial Theology in South Africa* (Cape Town: Longman).

Lutheran Church of Australia (2000). *Statement on Reconciliation* (Adelaide: LCA).

Lutheran Church of Australia (1997). Land, Justice and Settlement in Australia (Adelaide: LCA).

Lutheran Church of Australia (1997). *We're all people. Report and Recommendations of the Committee on Aboriginal Issues and Ministry, Lutheran Church of Australia.* (Adelaide: LCA).

Mudrooroo, Narogin (1986). *The Garden of Gethsemane. Poems from the Last Decade* (Melbourne: Hyland House).

Muhlhausler, Peter (2011). 'Herman Koeler's observations on South Australia in 1837 and 1838' in Peter Monteath (ed.) *Germans: Travellers, Settlers and their Descendants in South Australia* (Adelaide: Wakefield Press).

Pope, Marvin (1955). *El in the Ugaritic Texts* (Brill: Leiden).

Rainbow Spirit Elders (1997). *Rainbow Spirit Theology. Towards an Australian Aboriginal Theology* (Melbourne: Harper Collins).

Royal Commission into British Nuclear Tests in Australia (1985). *Report.* (Canberra: Australian Government Publishing Service).

Stephens, John (1988). *The Land of Promise* (Adelaide: Gillingham Printers).

Strehlow, T G H (1971). *Songs of Central Australia* (Sydney: Angus & Roberston).

Wilcken, John (1997). 'The Biblical Promised Land and Australian Aboriginal Peoples' in *The Australian Catholic Record*, lxxiv, pp. 86-98.